wild, wild world

SNAKES
AND OTHER REPTILES

Written by
Anita Ganeri

Illustrated by
James Field

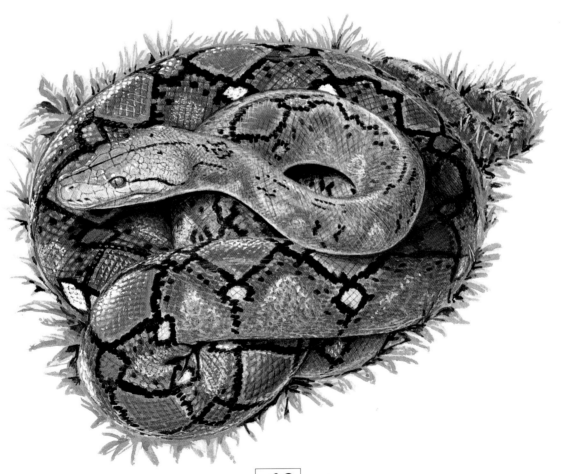

p

This is a Parragon Book
First published in 2001

Parragon
Queen Street House
4 Queen Street
Bath BA1 1HE, UK

Copyright © Parragon 2001

Produced by

David West ⚇ Children's Books
7 Princeton Court
55 Felsham Road
Putney
London SW15 1AZ

British Library Cataloguing-in-Publication Data

A catalogue record for this book is available from
the British Library.

ISBN 0-75254-668-6

Printed in Italy

Designer
Jenny Skelly
Illustrators
James Field
(SGA)
Rob Shone
Cartoonist
Peter Wilks
Editor
James Pickering
Consultant
Steve Parker

CONTENTS

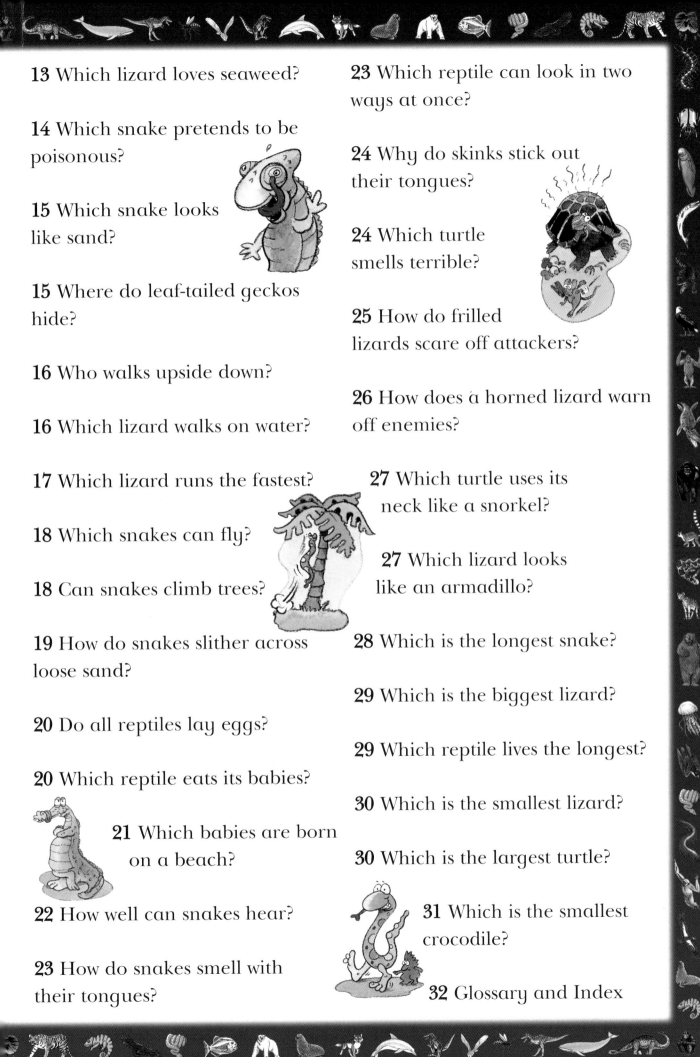

Snake

❓ What are reptiles?

Reptiles are a group of animals which includes snakes, lizards, turtles, tortoises, alligators and crocodiles. They are all vertebrates (they have bones and skeletons inside their bodies), they breathe air and most of them live on land. Their skins are scaly to stop their bodies drying out.

Lizard

Amazing! Lizards love sunbathing. All reptiles are cold-blooded. They can't control their own body temperature but rely on the weather instead. Cold lizards are sluggish and slow. So they warm up in the sun, then scurry off hunting.

Turtle

Which is the shortest snake?

At only about ten centimetres long, thread snakes are the shortest, thinnest snakes in the world. If you took the lead out of a pencil, they could slither through the hole. These rare snakes live in the West Indies, and eat tiny ants and termites.

Thread snake

Is it true?
Today's reptiles have famous relatives.

Yes. The relatives of today's reptiles were the dinosaurs, which ruled the Earth for more than 200 million years. They suddenly died out about 65 million years ago.

Which is the biggest reptile?

The biggest reptiles alive today are saltwater crocodiles. They're usually about four metres long, but a gigantic crocodile killed in 1957 measured no less than 8.64 metres, and weighed more than two tonnes.

Saltwater crocodile

Why do snakes shed their skin?

As a snake grows, its scaly skin gets too small. So the snake grows a new skin underneath, then slithers out of the old one, starting from the head and working down to the tail. A snake sheds its skin in one piece, several times a year.

6

Is it true?
You can tell a tortoise's age from its shell.

Yes. A tortoise's shell is made of bone, covered in tough, horny plates. The shell protects the tortoise's body. But that's not all it's good for. Each year, the plates grow a new ring. Count these up, and you can use them to estimate the tortoise's age.

Which reptile has armour plating?

Alligators and crocodiles are covered in tough, horny scales, strengthened with bone. This waterproof armour stops their bodies drying out in the sun, and protects them from enemies.

Reticulated python

Amazing! Geckos have see-through eyelids. These are clear flaps of skin which protect their eyes from dust and dirt. A gecko can't blink to clean its eyelids. So it sticks out its tongue and licks them clean.

Which snake uses a rattle?

The rattle at the tip of a rattlesnake's tail is made of hollow scales, loosely linked together. If an enemy gets too close, the rattlesnake shakes its rattle, which makes a loud, angry buzzing sound to scare the attacker away. If this doesn't work, the rattlesnake coils itself up, then strikes with its poisonous fangs.

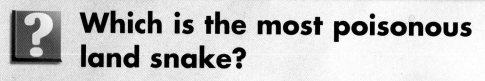

? Which is the most poisonous land snake?

Some of the deadliest land snakes live in Australia. A drop of their poison could kill 250,000 mice. Other highly dangerous snakes include cobras, rattlesnakes, and taipans, which can grow to 3.5 metres long.

8

? Which snake spits poison?

One type of cobra spits poison in its enemies' faces, blinding the victim! Spitting cobras have very good aims. They can hit a target more than two metres away.

Spitting cobra

Amazing! Fer-de-lance snakes have massive fangs and are deadly poisonous. They prey on rats and mice. Explorers claimed that local hunters in South America put these lethal snakes in tubes and fired them at their enemies.

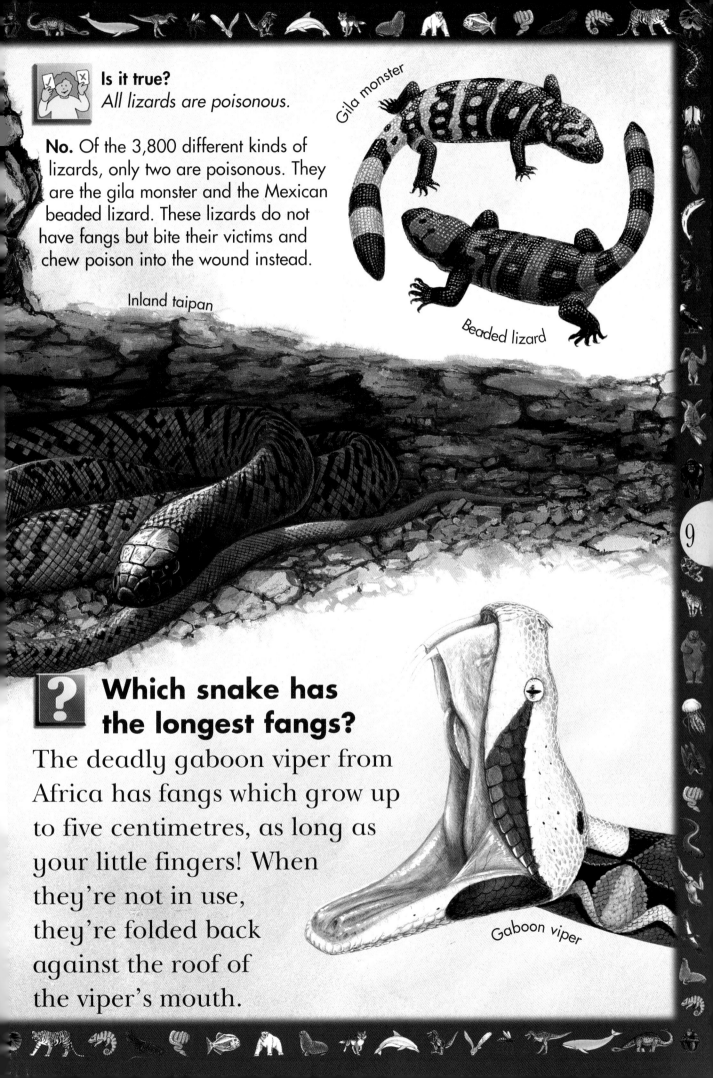

Is it true?
All lizards are poisonous.

No. Of the 3,800 different kinds of lizards, only two are poisonous. They are the gila monster and the Mexican beaded lizard. These lizards do not have fangs but bite their victims and chew poison into the wound instead.

Gila monster

Beaded lizard

Inland taipan

Which snake has the longest fangs?

The deadly gaboon viper from Africa has fangs which grow up to five centimetres, as long as your little fingers! When they're not in use, they're folded back against the roof of the viper's mouth.

Gaboon viper

？ What was the largest snake snack ever eaten?

The largest snack ever eaten by a snake was an impala antelope. It was devoured by an African rock python. The snake didn't chew its enormous meal into pieces. It swallowed the impala whole!

Rock python

Impala

？ Which snake squeezes its prey to death?

A boa constrictor holds its prey in its teeth, then wraps its coils tightly around it. The snake does not crush its victim to death but squeezes it until it suffocates.

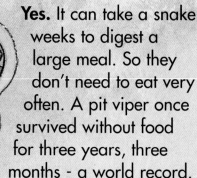

Is it true?
A snake can go for more than three years without food.

Yes. It can take a snake weeks to digest a large meal. So they don't need to eat very often. A pit viper once survived without food for three years, three months - a world record.

Why do snakes have elastic jaws?

A snake has sharp, backward-pointing teeth. Its teeth are good at holding food but can't bite it into chunks. Instead, snakes swallow their prey whole. Snakes have amazingly stretchy jaws, with elastic-like hinges between their jawbones. This means they can open their mouths very wide, to swallow food larger than the size of their heads, such as eggs.

11

Amazing! There are many scary stories of snakes swallowing people. But only a few of them are true. In 1979, a young boy in South Africa was seized by a 4.5 metre-long African rock python. His friends ran off to get help. When they came back about 20 minutes later, the snake had swallowed the boy whole.

Which lizard uses its tongue as a catapult?

A chameleon has a very long, sticky tongue. When it spots a tasty insect, it shoots out its tongue like a catapult, catches the insect and pulls it in. All in a split second.

Is it true?
Crocodiles don't like the taste of people.

No. Crocodiles do find people tasty, especially if they're hungry. It's estimated that saltwater crocodiles kill and eat up to 2,000 people each year.

Chameleon

Amazing! Alligators and crocodiles can snap their ferocious jaws shut with terrible force, but the muscles for opening their mouths up again are surprisingly weak. All you need to keep a crocodile's mouth shut is an elastic band. But keep your fingers away from those sharp, pointed teeth!

❓ Which lizard stores food in its tail?

The gila monster lives in the desert. It feeds on insects, birds' eggs and rodents. When there's plenty of food, it eats more than it needs and stores some as fat in its tail. It lives off this store when food is short.

Gila monster

13

❓ Which lizard loves seaweed?

The marine iguana lives on the Galapagos Islands. It loves eating seaweed. At low tide, it dives into the water and clings on to a weed-covered rock with its claws. It tears off the seaweed with its mouth.

Marine iguana

? Which snake pretends to be poisonous?

The milk snake lives in the rainforests of Central America. It's shy, secretive and harmless, but its bright bands of red, yellow and black make it look like the deadly coral snake. Its enemies think the milk snake is equally poisonous, and so leave it well alone.

14

Coral snake

Milk snake

Vine snake

Is it true?
Some snakes mimic vines.

Yes. The African vine snake hangs down from tree branches, looking just like a harmless vine. There's a nasty suprise for any bird that perches on it. It suddenly snatches the bird and swallows it down.

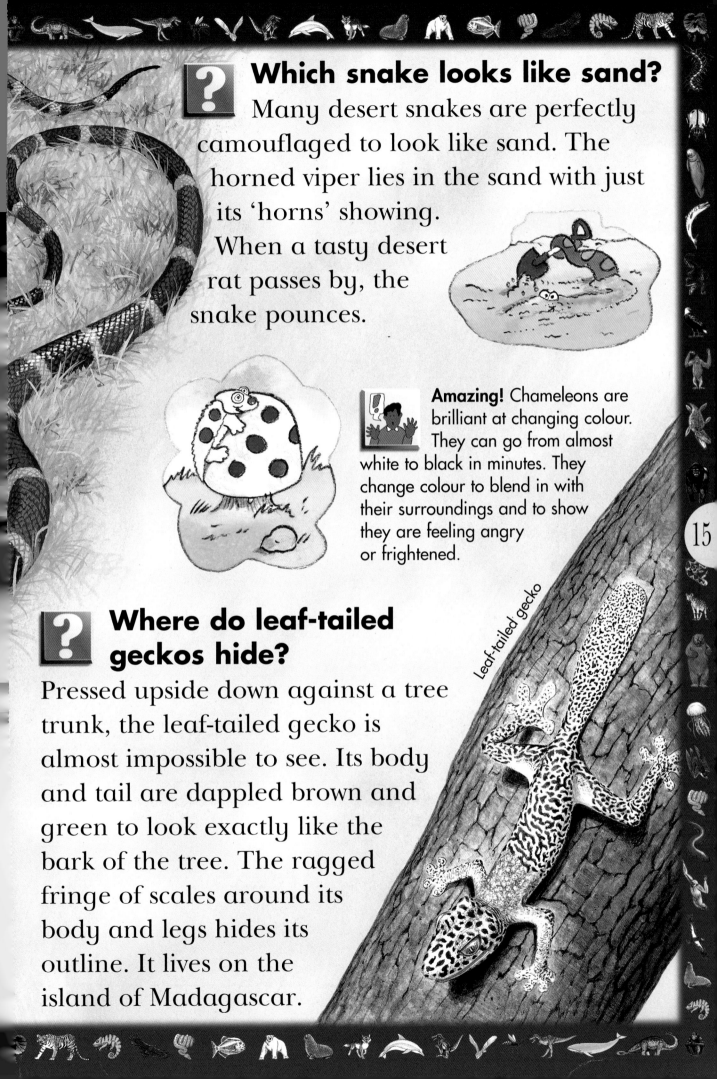

? Which snake looks like sand?

Many desert snakes are perfectly camouflaged to look like sand. The horned viper lies in the sand with just its 'horns' showing. When a tasty desert rat passes by, the snake pounces.

Amazing! Chameleons are brilliant at changing colour. They can go from almost white to black in minutes. They change colour to blend in with their surroundings and to show they are feeling angry or frightened.

? Where do leaf-tailed geckos hide?

Pressed upside down against a tree trunk, the leaf-tailed gecko is almost impossible to see. Its body and tail are dappled brown and green to look exactly like the bark of the tree. The ragged fringe of scales around its body and legs hides its outline. It lives on the island of Madagascar.

Leaf-tailed gecko

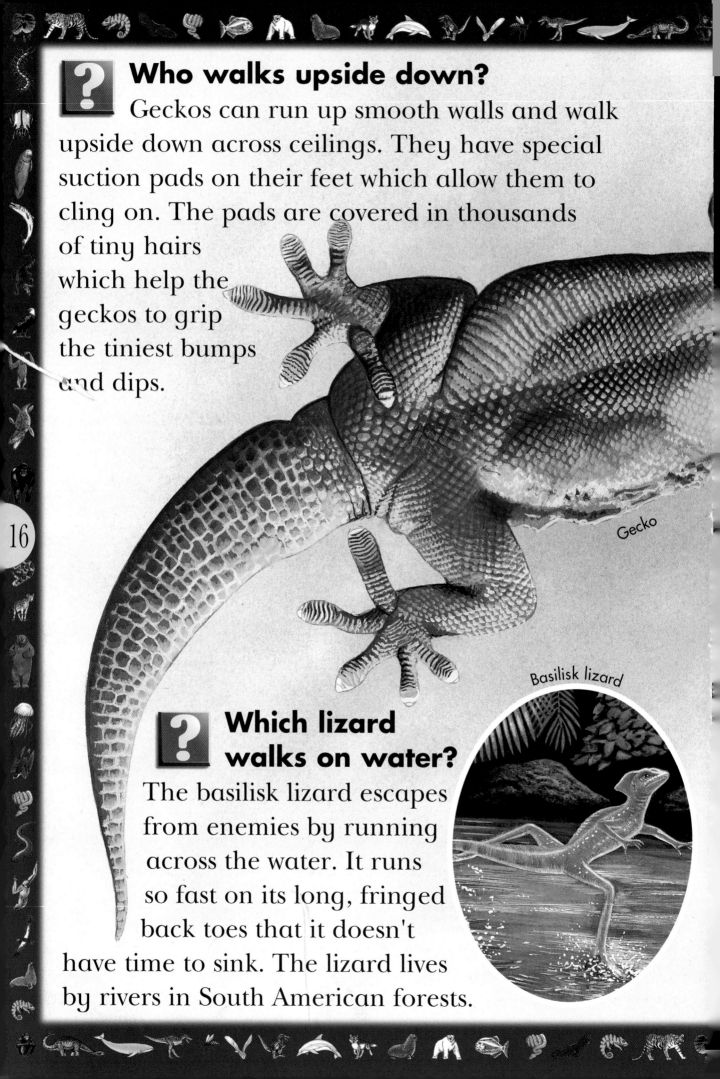

? Who walks upside down?

Geckos can run up smooth walls and walk upside down across ceilings. They have special suction pads on their feet which allow them to cling on. The pads are covered in thousands of tiny hairs which help the geckos to grip the tiniest bumps and dips.

Gecko

16

? Which lizard walks on water?

The basilisk lizard escapes from enemies by running across the water. It runs so fast on its long, fringed back toes that it doesn't have time to sink. The lizard lives by rivers in South American forests.

Basilisk lizard

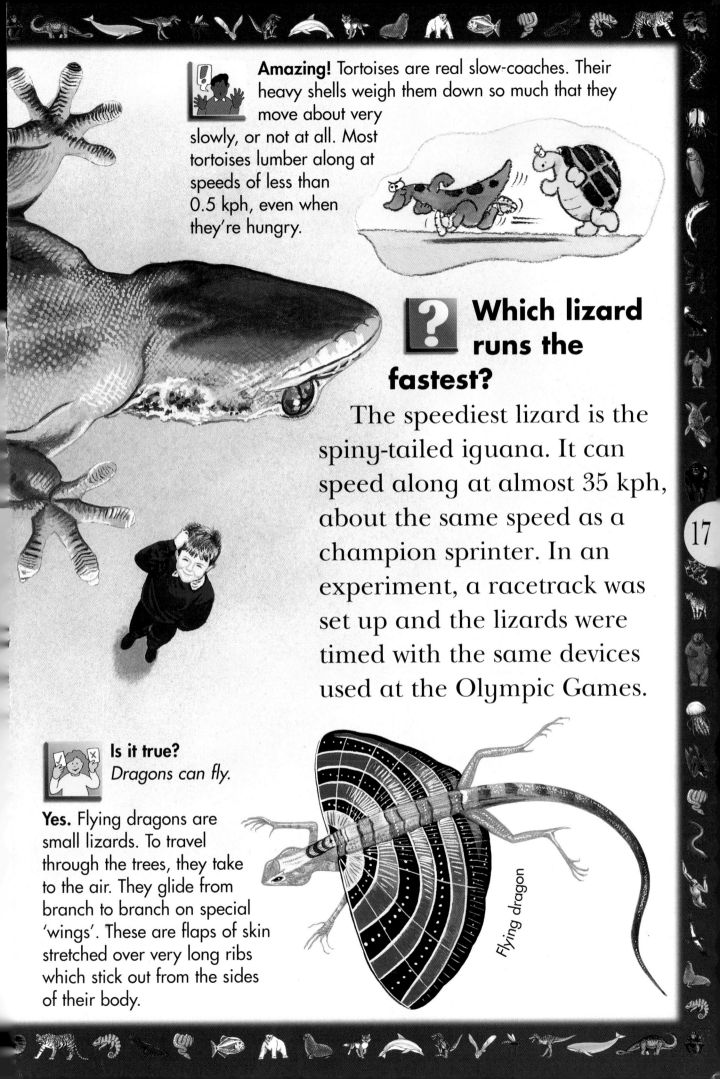

Amazing! Tortoises are real slow-coaches. Their heavy shells weigh them down so much that they move about very slowly, or not at all. Most tortoises lumber along at speeds of less than 0.5 kph, even when they're hungry.

❓ Which lizard runs the fastest?

The speediest lizard is the spiny-tailed iguana. It can speed along at almost 35 kph, about the same speed as a champion sprinter. In an experiment, a racetrack was set up and the lizards were timed with the same devices used at the Olympic Games.

17

Is it true?
Dragons can fly.

Yes. Flying dragons are small lizards. To travel through the trees, they take to the air. They glide from branch to branch on special 'wings'. These are flaps of skin stretched over very long ribs which stick out from the sides of their body.

Flying dragon

Which snake can fly?

The paradise flying snake can glide for 30 metres or more between the trees. It launches itself from a branch, using its tail to steer. Its body acts like a parachute, trapping air underneath, slowing it down as it floats down and lands on a lower branch.

 Amazing! The fastest land snake is the deadly black mamba. There are tales of them overtaking galloping horses. This isn't true but these speedy snakes can race along at about 20 kph.

Black mamba

Can snakes climb trees?

Many snakes slither through the trees, after birds and insects to eat. They are excellent climbers, with rough scales on the underside of their bodies to help them grip slippery branches.

Sidewinder

How do snakes slither across loose sand?

Sidewinders have an unusual way of slithering across loose, shifting sand. The sand makes it difficult to get a firm grip. So they flip their bodies sideways in a series of large loops. It leaves a tell-tale set of lines behind in the sand, like the tracks of a bulldozer.

19

Flying snake

Is it true?
Snakes once had legs.

Yes. The ancestors of snakes were lizard-like creatures with two pairs of legs. Snakes today do not have legs. Their skeletons are made of a skull, a long backbone and many pairs of ribs. This gives snakes a long, thin shape for slithering across the ground.

Do all reptiles lay eggs?

Most reptiles lay eggs with tough shells to protect the babies inside. But some types of snakes and lizards give birth to live young. When they are born, they look like miniature versions of their parents.

Which reptile eats its babies?

Large alligators only eat smaller ones during food shortages, and sometimes that includes their own young! When alligator babies hatch, their mother picks them up in her mouth and carries them safely to the water.

Alligator and young

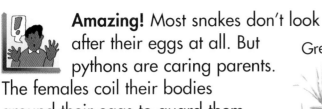

Amazing! Most snakes don't look after their eggs at all. But pythons are caring parents. The females coil their bodies around their eggs to guard them from attack. They also shiver and shake their coils slightly to keep the eggs warm.

Green tree python

Which babies are born on a beach?

Sea turtles come ashore to lay their eggs in nests on the beach. The female covers them with sand, then goes back to the sea. The eggs take about a month to hatch.

Green turtle

Is it true?
Baby green tree pythons are green.

No. Baby green tree pythons are yellow or red. They don't change colour to green until they're two years old.

21

Is it true?
Some geckos bark like dogs.

Yes. The barking gecko and the tokay gecko both bark like dogs. They use their loud voices to attract mates or defend their territory.

Spectacled cobra

? How well can snakes hear?

Snakes can't hear at all. They have no outer ears for detecting sounds. Instead, they pick up vibrations in the ground through their bodies. Snake charmers make it look as if a snake is dancing to the sound of music. But the snake is actually following the movement of the snake charmer's pipe with its eyes, ready to attack.

22

Amazing! Crocodiles and alligators are very noisy. They cough, hiss and bellow to attract mates and keep in touch with their group. The American alligator roars like a lion. It can be heard about 150 metres away.

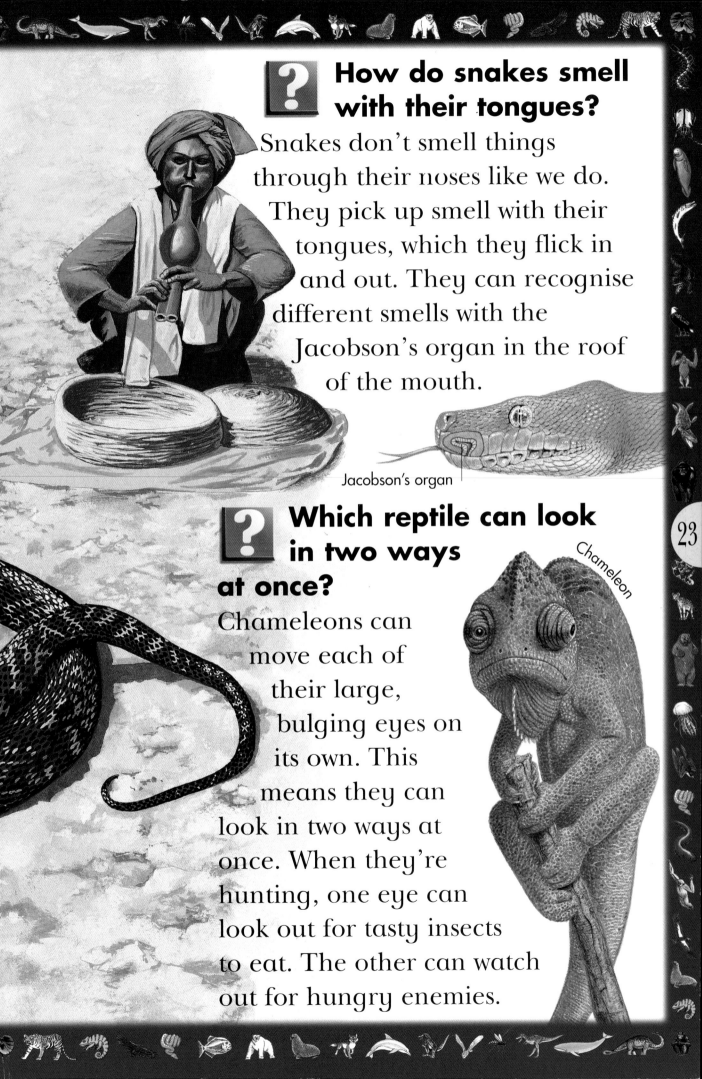

? How do snakes smell with their tongues?

Snakes don't smell things through their noses like we do. They pick up smell with their tongues, which they flick in and out. They can recognise different smells with the Jacobson's organ in the roof of the mouth.

Jacobson's organ

? Which reptile can look in two ways at once?

Chameleon

Chameleons can move each of their large, bulging eyes on its own. This means they can look in two ways at once. When they're hunting, one eye can look out for tasty insects to eat. The other can watch out for hungry enemies.

Blue-tongued skink

? Why do skinks stick out their tongues?

When a blue-tongued skink is threatened, it simply sticks out its bright blue tongue. Its enemies quickly run away. Skinks are types of lizards. The biggest skinks grow to over 60 cm, as long as your arm.

Hognosed snake

Is it true?
Hognosed snakes imitate rattlesnakes.

Yes. A hognosed snake has an ingenious way of protecting itself from enemies. It pretends to be a deadly poisonous rattlesnake. It rubs its tail against its body to make a sinister rattling sound. If this fails, the snake rolls on to its back and pretends to be dead.

? Which turtle smells terrible?

The tiny stinkpot turtle lives in North America. It spends most of its time in slow-moving streams. As well as its shell, the turtle has a secret weapon to use against its enemies. It gives off a truly terrible pong!

How do frilled lizards scare off attackers?

If a frilled lizard is chased into a corner, it puts on a dramatic show. It faces its attacker, with mouth wide open, and fans out the huge frill of skin around its neck. Then it sways from side to side, while hissing menacingly. It might look frightening, but in fact it's a fairly harmless lizard.

Frilled lizard

Amazing! If its tail is grabbed by an enemy, a lizard simply runs off and leaves its tail behind. The tail breaks off at a special weak spot between the tail bones. Luckily, the lizard can grow a brand-new tail, although it is often shorter than the old one.

Amazing! Water skinks have anti-freeze in their blood. Special chemicals stop their blood freezing even if the temperature falls below zero. This means that the skinks can come out of hibernation when there is still snow on the ground. Water skinks live in the mountains of eastern Australia.

? How does a horned lizard warn off enemies?

The horned lizard is an odd-looking reptile, covered in prickly spines. If it's attacked, it has a weird way of defending itself. It sprays blood from its eyes. This may fool its enemy into thinking it's wounded and leaving it alone.

Black rattlesnake

Horned lizard

Which turtle uses its neck as a snorkel?

Matamata turtle

The matamata turtle lives in slow-moving rivers in South America. It lurks on the riverbed, with its mouth wide open, waiting to snap up passing prey. It uses its long neck as a snorkel to hold its nostrils out of the water. In this way, it can breathe without having to swim up to the surface.

Is it true?
Crocodiles cry real tears.

Yes. Saltwater crocodiles look as if they are crying. But it's not because they are sad. They cry to get rid of extra salt which they take in with their food. People use the saying 'crocodile tears' to mean pretend tears.

Armadillo lizard

27

Which lizard looks like an armadillo?

The armadillo lizard has tough, armour-like skin on its head and back, just like a real armadillo. To escape from enemies, it hides in a crack in the rock, or it curls up into a tight, scaly ball to protect its soft stomach.

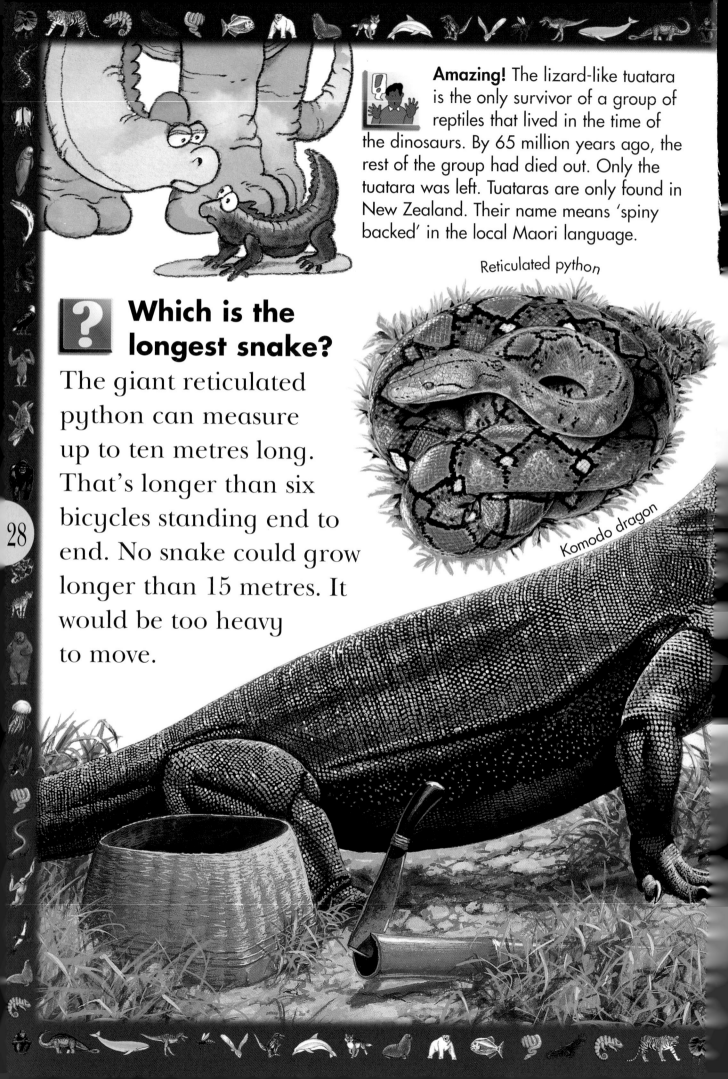

Reticulated python

? Which is the longest snake?

The giant reticulated python can measure up to ten metres long. That's longer than six bicycles standing end to end. No snake could grow longer than 15 metres. It would be too heavy to move.

Komodo dragon

Is it true?
Sea snakes are the most poisonous snakes.

Yes. All sea snakes are poisonous. One of the most poisonous of all is the banded sea snake from around Australia. Its venom is many times stronger than the deadliest land snake. Luckily, this snake rarely bites human beings.

Sea snake

Which is the biggest lizard?

The Komodo dragon is the world's largest lizard. Males can grow more than three metres long and weigh more than 150 kilograms. These record-breaking reptiles live on a few islands in Indonesia. They are meat-eaters and can swallow deer and pigs whole!

Which reptile lives the longest?

Tortoises live longer than any other animals on land. The oldest tortoise known was a Marion's tortoise from the Seychelles. When it died in 1918, it was thought to be over 150 years old.

29

Which is the smallest lizard?

A little gecko from the Caribbean is the world's smallest lizard. This tiny reptile is only about four centimetres long. That's about as long as your thumb.

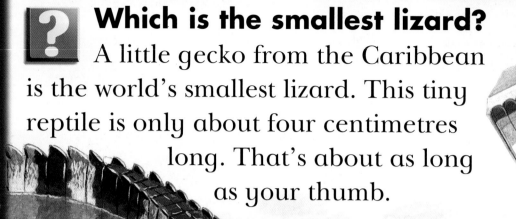

British Virgin Island gecko

Which is the largest turtle?

The leatherback turtle is about the size of a small car. This giant reptile can grow almost three metres long, from its head to the tip of its tail. It measures nearly three metres across its front flippers. It can weigh almost a tonne.

Leatherback turtle

Is it true?
Most poisonous snakes live in Africa.

No. Eight out of ten of the world's deadliest snakes live in Australia. About 3,000 people are bitten by snakes there every year. Luckily, very few of these snakebites are fatal.

Dwarf caiman

? Which is the smallest crocodile?

The smallest crocodile is the dwarf caiman which lives in South America. This mini crocodile only grows about 1.5 metres long, about a third of the size of its giant cousin, the massive saltwater crocodile.

Amazing! At almost a quarter of a tonne, the anaconda from South America is the world's bulkiest snake. This heavyweight snake lies in sluggish rivers or streams, waiting for prey to come down to drink. Then it grabs its victim in its mouth and squeezes it to death.

Glossary

Anti-freeze A chemical which prevents water, blood and other liquids from freezing solid.

Camouflaged To have a special colouring or pattern which makes an animal blend in with its background, making it very difficult to see, and less likely to be attacked by another animal.

Cold-blooded Animals which cannot control their own body temperature. Instead, they have to rely on the weather to warm them up or cool them down.

Fangs Special teeth through which snakes squirt poison into their enemies or prey.

Hibernation A deep sleep-like state which many warm and cold-blooded animals go into to survive through the winter.

Lethal Deadly, or fatal.

Maori The name for the native people of New Zealand and their language.

Prey Animals which are hunted and killed by other animals for food. To prey on means to catch prey.

Saltwater crocodile Also known as the Estuarine crocodile, they are the largest crocodiles, and can also live in fresh water.

Territory The patch of land or sea in which an animal lives. Many animals fiercely defend their territory.

Vertebrates Animals which have a spine inside their bodies. Vertebrates include mammals, birds, reptiles, amphibians and fish.

Index